S0-CPE-436

❖ **Why They Became Famous** ❖

ABRAHAM LINCOLN

❖ **Why They Became Famous** ❖

ABRAHAM LINCOLN

Lino Monchieri

Translated by Mary Lee Grisanti

Illustrated by Piero Cattaneo

Silver Burdett Company

ACKNOWLEDGEMENTS

We would like to thank David A. Williams, Professor Emeritus, Department of History, California State University, Long Beach and Diane Sielski, Library Supervisor, Coldwater Exempted Village Schools, Ohio for their guidance and helpful suggestions.

Library of Congress Cataloging in Publication Data

Monchieri, Lino.
  Abraham Lincoln.

  (Why they became famous)
  Translation of: Abraham Lincoln.
  Summary: Recounts the life of the dedicated man who survived a difficult childhood, became a country lawyer, and as sixteenth president of the United States guided the country during the Civil War.
    1. Lincoln, Abraham, 1809–1865 — Juvenile literature.
2. Presidents — United States — Biography — Juvenile literature. |1. Lincoln, Abraham, 1809–1865.
2. Presidents| I. Title. II. Series.
E457.905.M5713 1984   973.7'092'4 |B| |92| 84-51620
ISBN 0-382-06855-6   REV.
ISBN 0-382-06985-4 (Soft Cover)

© Fabbri Editori S.p.A., Milan 1981
Translated into English by Mary Lee Grisanti for Silver Burdett Company
from Perché Sono Diventati Famosi: Lincoln
First published in Italy in 1981 by Fabbri Editori S.p.A., Milan

© 1985 Silver Burdett Company. All rights reserved. Printed in the United States of America. Published simultaneously in Canada. This publication, or parts thereof, may not be reproduced in any form by photographic, electrostatic, mechanical or any other method, for any use, including information storage and retrieval, without written permission from the publisher.

CONTENTS

The Indiana Farm

In December of 1816 Thomas Lincoln moved his family from Kentucky to Indiana in hopes that life might be better for them there. Although Tom was by trade a master carpenter, he sought the dream of the farmer—to support his family successfully by living off his own land. He had bought and sold several properties before he sold the land near Hodgensville, Kentucky to move to Indiana. He was always looking for that one special place where he and his family could live out his dream—dependence on no one.

Thomas was an expert hunter. While tracking wild boar along the Ohio River he had discovered a plot of land that he thought might finally be the right place to stake his claim and settle with his wife and children.

When Tom and his wife Nancy left their log cabin in Kentucky, where their two children Abraham and Sarah had been born, they thought they were moving for the last time. Tom was used to hardships. It was without regret that he packed their few belongings into the wagon and headed down the road toward their new life.

For four days in the cold of winter they traveled over the bumpy, winding paths that led west. Finally they came to the Ohio River, and there they boarded a ferry. When the ferryman set them down on the opposite bank, they were in Indiana. Tom, with the experienced eye of a hunter, easily found the land again that he had chosen and showed it to his family with pride. "All this is ours, it's been measured and registered with the Land Office."

"But this is just a forest," Nancy objected fearfully. "There are no other families or farms for miles around!"

"It always begins like this," Tom reassured her. "The trees we clear for farming will be the logs we use to build our new house. The forest will provide us with plenty of wild game, nuts, and fruits to eat until our first crops come in." Still, in spite of Lincoln's optimism, it could not have been easy to keep his family well-fed during the winter months, and on into the spring and summer when they could expect their first harvest.

Abe Lincoln was only seven when his family left Kentucky. But he was already able to do many of the chores that his father did. He had inherited his father's deep love of the land and for all the plants and animals living there. Above all, he had inherited his father's ability to work hard and be proud of it. Abe worked along with the other members of his family to prepare their land for farming.

The Lincoln family spent the winter in a lean-to with only three sides. Tom had hastily built it to shelter them from the cold winds and heavy snows. Life could not have been comfortable or easy for them that winter. There was just no way the lean-to could have afforded them complete protection from the elements. They had to keep a fire going day and night to keep warm. The closest source of water was a mile away.

It was not until spring had arrived that they were able to begin cutting down the trees they would need to build a real cabin. Abe could handle an axe very well; in this he was much like his father, for the elder Lincoln was an expert woodsman.

The one thing in which Abe could not manage to imitate his father, no matter how hard he tried, was hunting. Even though he understood that wild game was essential to their very survival, Abe still could not make himself pull the trigger once he had an animal in his sights. He could find game and track it, but when it came time to shoot, something always made him stop.

Only once had Abe managed to pull the trigger, and kill a wild turkey. As he watched the creature fall to the ground and bleed to death his emotions churned inside him.

"Pa," he turned to his father, "can one shot like that kill a man?"

His father nodded, "Yes."

"Have you ever killed a man?" Abe asked.

"No."

"Have you ever seen a man get shot?"

"Yes," Tom told him sadly. "I saw my own father die from a gunshot wound. His name was Abraham, just like yours."

"How did it happen?"

His father looked away. "I'll tell you all about it later," he said. "Right now we have to get back home. Your mother will need some time to prepare your first catch so we can have it for dinner."

When they returned to their cabin they stopped for a moment to look at it and admire the results of their hard work. They had built every inch of the cabin with their own hands. Tom and Abe had cut down the trees to make the logs. Nancy and Sarah had helped by peeling the bark away to make the logs smooth. Together they had all helped to drag the logs to the spot upon which they had decided the cabin was to be built.

Inside, the cabin was large and spacious, with a beaten clay floor and a fine stone fireplace that heated the whole cabin evenly. Every table, chair, and chest had been handmade of wood from their trees. The mattresses on their beds were stuffed with dry leaves.

"What a house!" Tom said to his son with pride as they looked at their new home.

"It's nothing like the old lean-to we spent the winter in," Abe said.

"No, indeed. This house will last for centuries!"

"What will happen to our old lean-to now?" Abe asked.

"Well, when your mother's relatives, the Sparrows, get here from Kentucky with your cousin Dennis Hanks it will be fine for them to use for awhile.

"Hooray! We're going to have company!" Abe exclaimed.

"That's just what your mother said..." Abe's mother had missed the companionship of other women.

"They're going to need a better house than the lean-to won't they?"

"That's right. And when the time is right, we'll help them build it."

"Good," smiled Abe.

"And maybe your cousin can teach you some things about hunting."

"Ugh. I don't want to ever kill anything again. I just hate it, Pa."

"Well, I don't notice that you hate it when it gets to the dinner table..." Tom put his arm around his son's shoulder and the two walked into the cabin together.

All evening long Abe was burning with impatience. His father had promised to tell him the story of what had happened to grandfather Abraham. Abe could hardly sit still, but he waited for the right moment to approach his father. When he saw his father sit down in front of the fire after dinner to smoke his pipe, he grabbed his sister and they sat down right in front of him.

"We're ready, Pa!" he said.

"Ready for bed?" his father teased him.

"No! Ready for the story you promised us."

Thomas blew a smoke ring into the air. "Oh well, I knew that some day I would have to tell you.

"My family was living in Kentucky then. One day my father Abraham and my brothers Joshua and Mordecai were working in the fields. I was too little to help with the plowing so I just tagged along behind them, watching everything they did so I could learn."

"What were you learning, Pa?" asked Sarah.

"I was learning how to handle the horses—how to guide them so that the furrows would be plowed straight across the field. It's very hard to learn to control the reins and direct the plow at the same time. That day your grandfather was doing the plowing.

"Suddenly a shot rang out. It was as loud as thunder. My father raised his hand to his head and silently fell to the ground. My brothers ran into the house quicker than anything. I was alone. I walked toward my father, crying out his name. The blood pouring out of his wound into the freshly plowed earth frightened me. Suddenly I saw a huge Indian standing there. He was very fierce looking, with paint on his face and a crown of feathers on his head. He watched me without saying a word. I remember his eyes, it seemed like they were on fire. I stepped back. The Indian's lips moved as if he was about to say something, but I never heard what he had to say because another shot rang out. The Indian stiffened and fell straight to the ground like a bird shot in midair. My brother Mordecai had shot him from the window of our house. He had run there with Joshua to get his gun."

"Were you afraid, Pa?" Sarah asked.

"Well, I've never forgotten that day. Right before my eyes not one but two men died violently. And death didn't miss me by more than a hair's breath."

"Why did that Indian want to kill Grandpa?" Abe asked.

"I don't know," his father told him. "Maybe just out of pure hate for the white men who had taken the Indians' land. Or maybe to avenge another Indian's death."

"Did any Indians ever come back again to get you?"

"No, never again. But from that day on, Mordecai just couldn't get Indians off his brain. He'd kill any Indian who ever came into the sights of his gun."

Abe bowed his head thoughtfully. After his father had finished the story, he got up and said good night to everyone. Abe went off to bed where he lay awake thinking for a long time.

The next year Tom and Betsy Sparrow came to Indiana. They had been Nancy Lincoln's childhood guardians. They came from Kentucky with their nineteen-year-old nephew Dennis Hanks dreaming, as Thomas Lincoln had, of building their own home and living off the land through their own hard work.

But luck was against them. Not long after they arrived a deadly disease, known as the milk sickness, began to spread throughout that part of the country. The Sparrows were stricken by it and died just a few days after becoming ill.

The disease was relentless. First the Sparrows felt aches and pains all over their bodies. Then came a burning fever which left their arms and legs icy cold. Finally their tongues swelled and they were gripped by an unquenchable thirst. Within a short time of one another, they died in horrible pain. Their nephew Dennis moved in with the Lincolns.

But there was to be yet another victim. When a woman on a nearby farm became ill Nancy Lincoln went to take care of her. It was only a few days later when Nancy, the brave and wise wife of Thomas Lincoln, came down with the same dreadful symptoms herself. For seven long days she suffered. All during these days, Thomas kept the children away from her for fear they too would be infected. Finally he gave up and let them go to her bedside to say goodbye. With agonizing restraint, he tried to prevent the children from hugging her and kissing her as she lay dying. In the end though, he couldn't help but let them.

The next day they buried her in a clearing in the forest, alongside the fresh graves of Tom and Betsy Sparrow, whose fortunes had not improved with their move to the West.

One cannot say that Abraham Lincoln's childhood was the model of happiness and serenity that we expect for children today. His early life was full of all kinds of hardships that came in a new land where nature was wild and sometimes hostile, and where amenities like doctors and medical supplies were not yet common. But the hard work which he grew used to, and the terrible loss of his young mother, taught Abe lessons that he was to remember all his life.

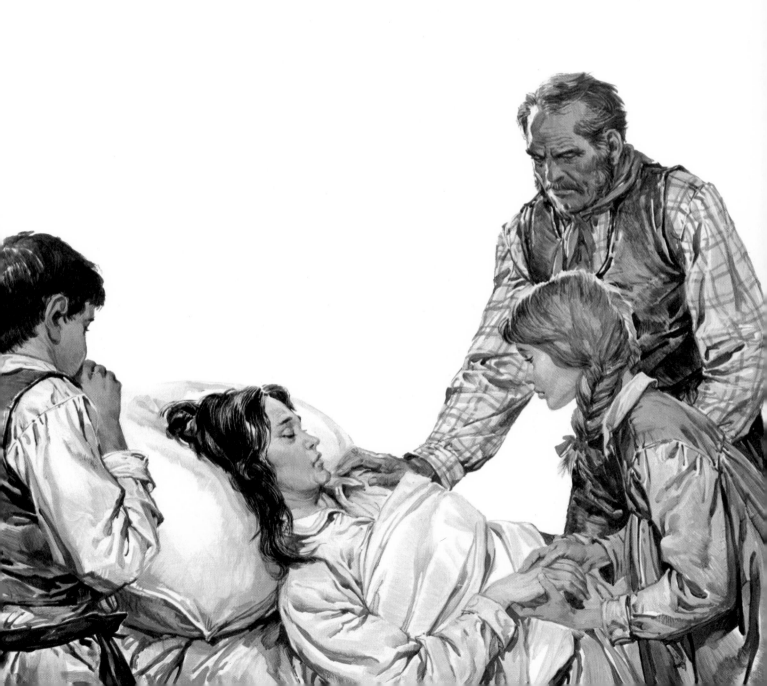

Learning to Read and Write

Life on the Indiana farm became harder. Young Sarah had to take on the chores her mother had done. She cooked the meals, mended the clothes and kept the cabin tidy. Thomas Lincoln, Abraham, and Dennis Hanks took care of the horses, cows, and pigs. They plowed the fields, sowed the seeds, and harvested the crops. Often there were disappointments to cope with. Once when the three had just been through the labor of plowing and planting, a flash flood poured over their land and washed the seeds away. The plowing and planting had to be done all over again.

Wild animals lurked in the woods all around the cabin—panthers, bears, wildcats, rattlesnakes. Lincoln wrote a verse explaining the dangers of life in Indiana when it was still part of the western frontier:

When first my father settled here,

'Twas then the frontier line

The panther's scream filled nights with fear

And bears preyed on the swine.

The Lincoln family was always pinched for money. Years later a friend named John Locke Scripps asked Presidential candidate Abraham Lincoln what his boyhood had been like. Lincoln responded: "Why Scripps, it is a great piece of folly to attempt to make anything out of my early life. It can all be condensed in a single sentence and that sentence you will find in Gray's *Elegy*—'The short and simple annals of the poor.'"

Family life changed tremendously in 1819, when Thomas Lincoln married for a second time. His new wife was Sarah Bush Johnston, a widow with three children of her own, two daughters, Elizabeth and Matilda, and a son named John. Sarah Johnston brought with her boxes of hats, dresses and other finery, things Sarah Lincoln had never seen before. Also, Sarah Johnston had a little money, and she used it to improve the life of the Lincoln family.

The cabin had become run-down since the death of Nancy Hanks Lincoln. Sarah Bush Johnston Lincoln set to work to make life more comfortable. She added furniture and put curtains on the windows.

She was more like a real mother than a stepmother to her husband's children. She took over the household burdens that young Sarah Lincoln had tried to manage by herself. And she provided young Sarah with prettier dresses than Thomas Lincoln had been able to afford.

Sarah Bush Johnston Lincoln was the first to recognize that there was something unusual about her stepson.

"I believe Abe is destined for greatness," she said to the boy's father. "He is so intelligent and he has so much character."

"I hope you're right," her husband replied. "I'd like to think that Abe has a better future than scratching a living from the land like I've had to do."

Abraham Lincoln never forgot how much his stepmother did for him. In later life he referred to her as "my angel mother." She lived to know that her opinion of Abraham Lincoln was right. She lived to see him in the White House.

The new Mrs. Lincoln brought a number of books with her, including her *Bible*. She encouraged Abe to read them, and reading became one of his strongest habits. Many a night he lay on the floor of the cabin reading the Scriptures by the light of flickering candles. Or, he would turn to exciting fiction like *Robinson Crusoe* and *The Arabian Nights*.

Abe's stepmother also insisted that he be given some schooling. She sent him to three different schoolmasters who taught pupils reading, writing, and arithmetic.

These were called "blab" schools because the pupils were compelled to study aloud. They spoke what they were thinking as they leaned over their copy books. If anyone stopped speaking, the schoolmaster assumed that the pupil concerned was not doing his lesson. And then a rod across the shoulders warned the pupil to concentrate.

This never happened to Abe Lincoln. He was so eager to learn that he was always ahead of his class in finishing his lessons.

One schoolmaster asked the class: "What do we do with wood?"

"We make things with wood," Abe answered. "We make fences and cabins and boats. We carve things, like bookends and curtain rods.

"You are correct, Abe Lincoln," said the schoolmaster. "You have a way with words. I wouldn't be surprised if you become a writer some day."

Abe was the hero of the class after that.

Unfortunately he did not stay in school very long. He had to help his father on the farm. And so the chores ended his education after about a year.

Still, he had learned how to study. He went forward on his own. He kept a board on which he would solve problems in mathematics. When he finished one problem, he would shave the board down with a knife, and then go on to another problem.

Soon Abe made a lot of friends in the area. It was a great day for him when he discovered those who would loan him books. He often walked miles to borrow a copy of *Pilgrim's Progress* or Aesop's *Fables*. By borrowing, he was able to read Parson Weems' biography of George Washington, the Declaration of Independence, and the Constitution of the United States.

Often he would carry a book with him around the farm. When he had finished plowing a field or milking the cows, he would sit down and read a few pages.

Sometimes his father wondered if Abe was doing the chores properly. "Abe, I don't know how you have time for reading," Thomas Lincoln said.

"I work hard at the chores," Abe responded, "so I can make the time. Have a look. If I've shirked anything, I'll do it over."

Thomas Lincoln had to admit that Abe never shirked any job when there was work to be done on the farm.

Of course Abe's stepmother was very pleased when she saw him with a book. "Read as much as you can," she advised him. "The more you read, the more you will make of yourself."

Abe followed her advice. As the years passed, he became the best-read person in the area.

All the while he was working hard, not only on the farm but also at odd jobs whenever he could find them. He helped other farmers with their planting in the spring, and with their harvesting in the fall.

One job was with the owner of a ferry who took passengers across the Ohio River. This experience led Abe to build a small boat of his own. He thus became familiar with the river—with its currents, shallows, and rocks. He learned how to estimate the depth of the water and the strength of the wind as he rowed against it.

One day he saw a steamboat as it was raising anchor. Suddenly two men rushed down onto the bank of the river.

"Young man, can you catch that boat?" cried one of the men.

"We'll make it worth your while!" the other shouted.

"Jump in!" came the reply. "I'll put you aboard!"

The two jumped in. Lincoln pushed his boat away from the bank with an oar. Then he began to row out into the river with all his might. They got to the steamboat just as it was beginning to move. The two men climbed aboard. From the deck, they leaned over the rail and each tossed a silver half-dollar into Lincoln's boat.

That was the kind of money he had never been paid before. He said he "could scarcely credit that I, a poor boy, had earned a dollar in less than a day."

At this time Abe was a popular figure in his neighborhood. He liked the democracy he saw developing. The people of Indiana believed in equality, which was something he believed in more than anyone. He was always welcome because he had a gift of humor.

The richest man in the neighborhood was James Gentry, who ran a big store. Gentry and his customers used to gather around while Abe Lincoln sat on a cracker barrel and amused them with his jokes and stories.

Working on the River

Abe Lincoln worked for two years as a ferryman on the Ohio River. He ferried many passengers out to the stately steamboats that moved up the river to Cincinnati or down to the Mississippi and on to New Orleans.

One day James Gentry made him an offer.

"Abe, I have a cargo of corn and hogs I want to sell in New Orleans. My son Allen will be going. But you know how to handle a boat better than he does. I'd like you to take charge. What do you say?"

"I'd sure like to, Mr. Gentry," Abe responded enthusiastically. He was eager to see something of the big world south of the frontier where he had lived all his life.

He and Allen Gentry built a flatboat. Loading their cargo aboard, they floated down the Ohio to the place where it meets the broad Mississippi, America's greatest river. The Mississippi carried them swiftly downstream. They traveled during the day and tied their boat to trees on the riverbank at night so they could get a few hours of sleep.

One night Abe was awakened by a stealthy sound coming toward them. Quickly he roused Allen Gentry.

"Thieves!" he whispered. "Get ready!"

Several men emerged from the woods and tried to board the flatboat. But Abe and Allen put up a fight and drove them off.

Continuing their trip, Abe and Allen reached New Orleans. There they sold their cargo and bought some drygoods for Gentry's store back in Indiana. They also sold their flatboat, knowing that they could not row back up the Mississippi. They would have had to row more than a thousand miles to get home.

This visit to New Orleans had a strong effect on Abe Lincoln. He saw a big city for the first time. He was amazed at the number of ships tied up along the waterfront—some of them ocean-going vessels from foreign ports. He saw huge bales of cotton on the wharves, and heard the clink of gold coins as the bales changed hands.

There were many foreign people in New Orleans. Abe and Allen heard French, Spanish, and Portuguese spoken as they walked around New Orleans.

Allen pointed to some big houses in the fashionable part of the city. "Abe, they must be rich people who live there," he commented.

"Yes, but there are a lot of poor people who work for them. I wonder why so few have so much, and so many so little in this life."

That question continued to haunt Abe Lincoln. He had always been poor, and he knew the suffering of the poor. Most of all he sympathized with the slaves who toiled for their masters.

Abe and Allen returned to Indiana. James Gentry was highly satisfied with Abe's handling of the mission to New Orleans.

"I knew I could rely on you," said the store owner. "Here's twenty-four dollars."

"That's a lot of money, Mr. Gentry."

"Well, you earned it. You've showed me how to get my cargoes to New Orleans. My business will be a lot more profitable in the future."

This was Lincoln's first important success. He would have many more. But he didn't know that at the time. He still had to work hard to make a living.

Following his trip to New Orleans, Abe went back to work as a ferryman on the Ohio River. He took passengers into the middle of the river to board steamboats. And he ferried travelers across the river between Indiana on the northern bank and Kentucky on the southern bank.

In crossing the river, he accidentally broke the law. He had never taken out a license to be a ferryman because Indiana did not require a license. Unknown to him, Kentucky did require a license. Without knowing it, he broke the law every time he landed travelers on the Kentucky shore or picked them up there.

An unscrupulous rival ferryman, jealous of Abe's success on the river, had him brought before a judge. Abe was released on his promise to ferry passengers only to the steamboats in the river, not to Kentucky.

This was his first experience with a law court. He felt intrigued, and wanted to learn more about America's legal system. Within a few years he began to study the law seriously. And he went to court and listened to cases whenever he could to see how the guilt or innocence of defendants was decided.

Meanwhile, the Lincoln family moved again. Thomas Lincoln felt that he could not make a success in Indiana. He decided to go west. He consulted his son, who was now twenty-one.

"Abe, I hear good things about Illinois from your cousin, John Hanks. I'd like to give it a try. Farming here hasn't got us very far."

"There's plenty of land in Illinois," Abe agreed. "And John Hanks is a good judge of farmland. Let's go."

In 1830 the Lincolns piled their belongings on three wagons and set out for Illinois, to the west across the Indiana border. Thomas Lincoln drove the best wagon, which was drawn by horses. Abe and Dennis Hanks each drove a lumbering vehicle pulled by a team of oxen. This caravan of the three wagons was painfully slow, covering only a few miles a day. And the family's destination was two hundred miles away!

Getting there was a struggle. There were no highways or paved roads to travel along. They had to make their way through the woods. Occasionally they came to a trail made by Indians or white hunters. Then the going was easier. But that wasn't very often.

When they came to wide streams, Abe and Dennis searched along the banks for a ford. Much time was lost in this way. But they got across every stream.

When it rained, the animals plodded through heavy mud while the drivers cracked their whips and pulled on the reins. Thomas Lincoln led the way in his horse-drawn wagon. Then came Dennis Hanks in his ox-cart. And last came Abe in his ox-cart. He was last so he could keep an eye on the others ahead of him.

They finally reached Decatur near the Sangamon River—where they met John Hanks. The men built another log cabin. The women did what they could to make it comfortable.

This was Abe Lincoln's introduction to Illinois, the state where he would make a name for himself—and start along the path that would lead him to the White House. But all this was in the future as he helped the others clear the land and plant the first crop in their new home.

In order to make some money quickly, Abe hired himself out with his ox. A number of newly arrived farmers along the Sangamon River needed fences around their land. These fences showed where one farmer's acres ended and his neighbor's began. The fences also kept livestock from wandering off their owner's farm onto somebody else's.

The fences were made of posts in the ground with long rails in between. Splitting rails was a back-breaking job. It involved chopping trees down, cutting the branches off, and splitting the trunks lengthwise. Many farmers hired rail splitters to do the work for them. A number who lived near the Lincoln farm hired Abe. He split around two thousand rails, and earned the title by which he became known—"Abe Lincoln, the Rail Splitter."

Abe made many friends in the Sangamon River area. One of them was Denton Offutt, a businessman from Springfield. Offutt intended to increase his profits by trading down the Mississippi to New Orleans. He needed somebody to take charge, and he decided on Abraham Lincoln.

"Abe, I've heard you tell stories about your trip down the Ohio and the Mississippi. How about making a trip with my cargo? This time you can skip the Ohio. The Sangamon flows into the Illinois River, and the Illinois flows directly into the Mississippi. You'll be downriver from the Ohio all the way."

"Sounds fine to me, Mr. Offutt. I'll take my relatives, John Hanks and John Johnston, with me. Where's your boat?"

Offutt looked startled. "Gosh, I never thought of that! I've got a cargo but no boat!"

"Don't worry. We'll take care of that. We'll build you a boat."

Lincoln, Hanks, and Johnston set up a rough lean-to on the Sangamon River while they were at work. The other two agreed that Abe should be their cook. They went out hunting, leaving Abe behind because he did not like to shoot animals. While they were gone, he felled trees and cut them into logs. When they returned, he prepared meals of the turkeys, rabbits, and deer they brought back from the woods.

They floated their logs down to a sawmill to be cut into planks. There they spent a month building their boat. It was in the shape of an oblong, and could be steered by two long oars, one near the front and one at the rear. It was large enough to hold the barrels, bales, and crates filled with merchandise such as corn and coon skins. There were also hogs in cages for delivery at the mouth of the Mississippi.

The great moment came. The three went aboard, along with Offutt, who wanted to see how they made out on the first leg of the voyage.

Disaster nearly struck at New Salem. They tried to float with the current over a dam. But the water was too shallow, and they got stuck on top of the dam. Water was flowing in over the stern.

"What'll we do, Abe?" John Hanks asked anxiously.

"We'll have to take part of the cargo out to lighten the boat. Then we'll bore a hole in the stern to let the water out. After that we'll plug the hole, ease the boat over the dam, and reload the cargo."

The plan worked. Offutt complimented Abe for being so clever. The businessman waved good-by from the bank as Lincoln, Hanks, and Johnston drifted downstream and out of sight.

The Slave Market

When the flatboat reached New Orleans, Abe supervised the sale of its contents. He bought the goods Offutt wanted, sold the boat, and prepared for a return trip up the Mississippi on one of the steamboats headed north.

While waiting to board the steamboat, Abe showed John Johnston around the city. The younger man was impressed by most of what he saw.

Then they came to a number of human beings held together by chains. There were three men and two women. They all looked ill-treated. They all looked desperate.

Abe's face darkened. "If I ever get a chance to hit that thing," he told his companion, "I'll hit it hard."

"What do you mean by that?" John asked.

"Slavery. It's the worst thing in America. The slave trade is still going on, bringing in black people from Africa. And inside America, slave owners sell slaves as if they were livestock."

"Like when we sell horses and cattle?"

Abe nodded. "It's the same thing. This is the New Orleans slave market. Those slaves will be sold at auction to the highest bidders. They're chained together so they can't escape."

Disobedient slaves in other states were often transported down the Mississippi to be sold in the New Orleans slave market. Their new masters there put them to work on the cotton and sugar cane plantations. The work was brutally hard, and the mortality rate was high. The slaves died like flies. That was why the plantation owners needed more slaves all the time.

Slaves dreaded being sent to New Orleans. Their greatest fear was to be "sold down the river." We still use that phrase when we have been betrayed or mistreated by other people.

"Slavery is the big issue facing this nation," Abe commented. "It led to the Missouri Compromise."

"The Missouri Compromise? What was that?"

"Well, it was a measure accepted by the U.S. government in 1820. That was the year after your mother married my father. Maine was admitted to the Union as a free state. Missouri came in as a slave state. And slavery was prohibited in the Louisiana Purchase above the southern boundary of Missouri. But now slave owners are trying to get rid of that last provision. They want the right to take slaves anywhere in the lands President Jefferson bought from France—the Louisiana Purchase."

"Will the slave states win in Washington?" John asked.

"I don't know," Abe confessed. "But I'll tell you this. They won't win if I have anything to say about it. The Missouri Compromise won't last forever. We Americans will have to decide whether we want slavery to spread—or whether we want to keep it out of any more states that join the Union."

"We should all agree to stop it, shouldn't we?"

"That's easy to say, John. The trouble is that the economy of the South is based on slavery. The plantations couldn't keep going without gangs of slaves to work in the fields."

As Abe finished speaking, a crowd gathered around the platform of the slave market. An auctioneer climbed up the steps onto the platform. He ordered the slaves to be unchained. One by one he showed each one to the crowd.

"They're all hale and hearty!" he called out. "They're good for the hardest kind of work! Great bargains! Come on, now! What am I bid?"

Members of the crowd shouted out their bids. The three men and two women were quickly sold. Their new owners took them away. The slaves looked terror-stricken as they shuffled off.

John was horrified. "I've never seen slaves sold before!"

Abe shrugged. "That's because slavery isn't economical in the backwoods. Remember the hard time we've had

feeding ourselves? We couldn't afford to feed any slaves as well. But even the rich in the North don't want slaves. There are no plantations in the North for slaves to work on."

"I see, Abe. Northerners use hired hands instead of slaves. But hired hands work hard, too, don't they?"

"Of course, John. But at least they're free."

Posters advertising "Slaves for Sale" were fastened to the boards of the platform. Underneath the heading appeared descriptions of the individuals who could be purchased. Men were described as "suited for the hardest work" or "knows how to shoe horses." Women were described as "good cooks" or "experienced at picking cotton."

A young girl was pushed up onto the platform. The auctioneer gripped her by one arm and raised his hand in a signal for bids. Below the platform, her mother screamed and rushed forward to save her. A brutal overseer grabbed the mother and forced

her back with a whip. The girl was sold and hustled away. The mother was left weeping, knowing she would never see her child again.

Abe turned to John. "Now do you understand the meaning of slavery?"

"I sure do, Abe. Something has to be done about it."

"Something will be done. But what it is, I just don't know."

The two had seen as much of the slave market as they could stand. They walked away and strolled through the streets of New Orleans. Eventually they returned to the docks. The steamboat on which they had booked passage was getting up steam. They went aboard for the trip home.

The steamboat pulled away from the docks into deep water. It headed up the Mississippi. Abe and John listened to the rhythmical sound of the paddlewheel hitting the water at the stern.

During the trip home, John Johnston remarked: "I heard somebody say that cotton is king in the South."

"That's the heart of the matter," Abe Lincoln told him. "The South grows cotton and sells it abroad, mostly in England. The English need large amounts of cotton

for their spinning wheels. They spin the cotton into cloth and sell it. That's why there are so many plantations in the South where slaves pick cotton. The overseers keep them busy all day long. Slaves who don't pick enough cotton are often beaten with clubs."

"Somebody should tell their story," John observed.

Unknown to them, this would happen. In 1852 Harriet Beecher Stowe published her novel, *Uncle Tom's Cabin*. This famous novel is about life on a plantation in the South in the days of slavery.

It shows how slave owners lived in luxury while their black slaves did all the hard work. The slaves lived in squalid cabins. They slept on piles of straw, and they ate whatever was provided by the master of the plantation. Each morning most of them were forced to go into the fields and pick cotton. A few were lucky enough to work in their master's house.

Uncle Tom is the hero of the story. He is a black man who never loses his dignity in spite of the brutality to which he is subjected.

The villain of the story is Simon Legree, who is determined to make the slaves pick as much cotton as they possibly can. He and his assistants use whips and clubs to force men, women, and children to keep working for most of every day in the hot sun.

The villain has given us a name we use all the time. Anyone we think is too harsh with other people, we call "Simon Legree."

Harriet Beecher Stowe's novel became a best-seller. It was read all over America. Southerners condemned her for the harsh picture she drew of slavery in the slave states. Northerners admired her for portraying slavery as it really was. Thus, *Uncle Tom's Cabin* contributed to the debate over slavery. It helped bring on the Civil War by convincing Northerners that slavery was a horrible system that had to be ended.

Harriet Beecher Stowe visited the White House during the Civil War. President Abraham Lincoln greeted her as "the little lady who started the big war."

However, all this was in the future as Abe Lincoln sailed up the Mississippi after his second trip to New Orleans. He would have considered it ridiculous if somebody had predicted that one day he would be president of the United States.

"Abe, what are you going to do when we get back? John asked.

"Mr. Offutt offered me a job in his store in New Salem. I'll take it."

"Why don't you go into politics?"

"Maybe I will someday. But I'll need the support of the people."

John made a joke. "Why don't you ask Andy Jackson for his support?"

Abe laughed. "Andy Jackson will never hear of me. I'm only a dirt farmer from Illinois."

They were referring to President Andrew Jackson.

America was booming under Jackson's leadership. The free states were building their economies under the factory system. New wealth was being created by businessmen and bankers. Cities like Philadelphia, New York, and Boston were growing by leaps and bounds.

More and more people benefited from the Jacksonian system. In particular, the West began to share in the prosperity.

But Andrew Jackson did nothing for the slaves.

A New Course for America

Denton Offutt furnished his store in New Salem with the goods Abe Lincoln had bought for him in New Orleans. Abe worked in the store as a clerk. He sold groceries and clothing to the people of New Salem. Offutt paid him fifteen dollars a month.

A group of rowdy young men lived in the town. Their leader was Jack Armstrong, who disliked Abe for being so popular.

"Abe Lincoln, I challenge you to a wrestling match," said Jack Armstrong. "We'll see who's the strongest."

"Done!" Abe responded. He did not like violence, but he was never one to show the white flag if an opponent tried to frighten him.

When word of the wrestling match got around, many spectators flocked to the scene. Abe knocked Jack off his feet and quickly pinned his shoulders to the ground. Jack admitted defeat, and became one of Abe's best friends.

In 1832 the Indians who lived in western Illinois attacked the white settlers. Since the Indians were led by Chief Black Hawk, this was called the Black Hawk War.

Abe enlisted at once. His company elected him their captain, with Jack Armstrong as his sergeant. The company marched into the woods ready for battle. However, they saw no Indians except a peaceful old man. Lincoln protected him from the rest of the company who thought that "the only good Indian is a dead Indian." Abe never tolerated that kind of thinking.

After the Black Hawk War, Abe ran for a seat in the Illinois Legislature. He campaigned hard, making many a stump speech to the voters of his district. He lost the election, but he decided to run again when the time came.

Abe bought a store in partnership with William J. Berry. When the store failed and Berry died, Abe promised to make good on the debts for both of them. He worked hard and paid all the creditors. After that he was called "Honest Abe" by his fellow citizens in New Salem. The nickname stuck to him for the rest of his life.

In 1833 he was appointed the postmaster of New Salem. He handled all the mail that arrived at the post office. When he delivered the mail, he often carried letters in his hat. As postmaster, he got to know all the voters of New Salem. Most of them liked him. They helped him win a seat in the Illinois legislature in 1834.

Abe now began to study law in a serious way. He borrowed law books and spent his spare time mastering such things as Supreme Court decisions and the laws of the state of Illinois. On one occasion, a friend saw him lying on a woodpile with an open book in his hand.

"Abe, what are you reading? the friend inquired.

"I'm not just reading," came the reply. "I'm studying the law. I intend to become a lawyer."

Vandalia was the capital of Illinois at that time. Abe therefore went to Vandalia to attend the state legislature. He was a member of the Whig Party, which opposed the Democratic Party of President Andrew Jackson.

Abe opposed the Democrats because he believed Jackson was not doing enough to help the states, including Illinois.

"We need roads, bridges, and canals in our state," Abe told his colleagues in the Illinois House of Representatives. "President Jackson will not provide us with them. We will have to do the job ourselves."

So, he voted with the Whigs all during his time in Vandalia.

Although Abe Lincoln never had anyone to teach him the law, he learned enough by himself to pass the bar examination in 1836. When a young law student asked him the secret of success, Lincoln replied: "It isn't necessary to have a teacher. Do what I did. Get the law books you need to know, and study them. Always remember that your own determination to succeed is the most important thing."

Now a full-fledged lawyer, Lincoln took clients and appeared in court to defend them. He became known as a shrewd judge of evidence, one who could easily spot the strong points of a client's defense. Rival lawyers learned that he could also spot the weak points in their arguments.

He took cases in county courts, often riding for miles through the countryside to get there. He was the "prairie lawyer" of Sangamon County.

Lincoln met many people on these rides. He talked with them, and learned how they felt about the Illinois state government and the national government in Washington. This helped him to form his opinions about what ought to be done.

"We need a bridge over the river," said one farmer. "It's hard to get corn to market when we have to take our wagons all the way up to the ford."

"I'll do what I can to see you get your bridge at the next session of the legislature," Lincoln promised.

"I believe you," was the answer. "They don't call you 'Honest Abe' for nothing."

"I appreciate that," Lincoln said. "I'll do my best."

Back in Vandalia, he persuaded the other members of the state legislature to vote for the bridge. He rose to become a leader of the Whig Party in Illinois.

At that time he began to think of getting married. It has been said that one memory restrained him—the memory of Ann Rutledge.

Ann Rutledge was the daughter of a tavern keeper in New Salem. She was an attractive young lady with blue eyes and blonde hair. Abe Lincoln met her at the tavern. According to the story, he fell in love with her and wanted to marry her.

The story goes on to say that when Ann died in 1835, Lincoln was so distraught that his friends feared that he might commit suicide. The end of the story says that he cherished Ann's memory for the rest of his life.

Edgar Lee Masters, the American poet, made Ann one of his characters in his *Spoon River Anthology*. Masters makes her say from the grave:

I am Ann Rutledge who sleeps beneath these weeds,
Beloved of Abraham Lincoln,
Wedded to him, not through union,
But through separation.

The story is an intriguing one. The only trouble is that there is no reason to believe it. Lincoln himself never mentioned a romance with Ann Rutledge. That he hoped to marry her is a legend started by somebody in New Salem nearly thirty years later when he was President of the United States. Early Lincoln biographers repeated the story, and it became a part of Lincoln folklore. Today no scholar believes it. Still, the story about Abraham Lincoln and Ann Rutledge persists.

In 1837 Springfield replaced Vandalia as the capital of Illinois. Abraham Lincoln, as a member of the state legislature, moved to Springfield. There he met a visitor from Kentucky named Mary Todd.

Mary came from a genteel family. She loved dancing, played the piano, and knew French. She was quite a contrast to lanky, rugged Abe Lincoln with his rough country manners. Their friends doubted that she would ever take him seriously. They thought she was better suited to Stephen A. Douglas, the leading Democratic politician in Illinois.

"Mary, Mr. Lincoln was raised in the backwoods!" her sister protested.

"Maybe so, but there's something about him that tells me he will make his mark in the world."

"Do you think he will be a success in politics?"

"Yes. He may even be President some day."

Her sister chuckled. "I see what you mean. You will be the First Lady."

"Don't be surprised if that happens."

Abraham Lincoln married Mary Todd on November 4, 1842. They bought a house in Springfield, and lived there until they made their trip to Washington in 1861. As she had guessed, they lived in Washington as President and First Lady.

They had four sons. Abraham Lincoln was a good father who showed his children much affection. Mrs. Lincoln had a quick temper that made her difficult to live with. But she and her husband got along as well as most married couples.

Honest Abe

In 1846 Abraham Lincoln was elected as a representative from the state of Illinois to the United States Congress. His rival, Stephen Douglas, had become a senator from Illinois and it seemed that he was on the road to the Presidency.

After completing his term, Abe did not run again. He returned home to Springfield, much to the distress of his wife Mary, who had had dreams of one day living in the White House. She could not hide her disappointment and continually expressed her disapproval of his outspokenness.

It is no mystery why Lincoln did not run for a second term in Congress. He was just too outspoken, and his stand had made him unpopular in his home state. He had joined other members of the Whig party in attacking and blaming President James Knox Polk for provoking a war against Mexico.

This was a courageous stand for Lincoln to take since the war had gained a great deal of support among the patriotic land-hungry citizens of his home state. Lincoln felt that opposing the war was the right thing to do, but remaining true to his principles had not furthered his political career.

In Congress, and throughout the nation, the subject of slavery was quickly becoming an issue and cause for much debate. Abe supported several measures to prohibit its spread, and this also limited his popularity in certain circles.

When his term was over he retired from political activity for five years and threw his energies into his law practice with renewed vigor. His reputation grew among his colleagues and constituents.

Making the most of this new control over his time, Lincoln traveled throughout the fifteen electoral districts of Illinois, practicing law. His patience and integrity as a lawyer served to bring his political ideas to people who might never have had an opportunity to hear them otherwise.

It was at this time that Abe became involved in a celebrated legal case. He was called upon to defend a poor man named Duff Armstrong, Jack Armstrong's son, who had been accused of murder. Duff seemed to represent all the weak creatures of this earth who have been unjustly accused of wrongdoing.

Lincoln was very successful with this case, and because of this his reputation was spread far and wide. Refuting some false testimony Abe upheld that:

"The witness insists on his version. He left the alley, long after midnight, in the light of a full moon bright enough to show every detail of the killing. But, gentlemen of the court, I have here an almanac and it shows clearly that on the night in question only a quarter moon had shined. Gentlemen of the jury! We cannot assume that because this man is poor and uneducated, hungry and desperate for money, that he is the one who committed this crime. I submit to you that among the poor there are also good men and bad men, honest men and liars. My client is an honest man who has been unjustly accused." On the first ballot, Duff Armstrong was acquitted.

While Abraham Lincoln practiced law in Springfield, the Whig Party was breaking up. The Kansas-Nebraska Act of 1854, introduced by Senator Stephen A. Douglas, said that slavery in those territories should be decided by the people who lived there. It was passed after a bitter debate in Congress.

The Kansas-Nebraska Act destroyed the Missouri Compromise, which prohibited slavery above the southern boundary of Missouri. Kansas and Nebraska were both above the southern boundary of Missouri.

Douglas carried the northern Democrats with him. But the Whig Party broke up into the Cotton Whigs (for slavery) and the Conscience Whigs (against slavery). A number of Conscience Whigs, anti-slavery Democrats, and Free Soilers founded the Republican Party in 1854 to oppose the extension of slavery. Lincoln joined the Republican Party two years later.

In 1858 he ran against Douglas for a seat in the U.S. Senate. During that summer and fall, the two men confronted one another in the historic Lincoln-Douglas debates.

There were seven debates in different places around Illinois. The issue was whether the people of Kansas and Nebraska had a right to hold slaves if they chose to do so. Douglas said "yes" and Lincoln said "no" to that question. Lincoln's point was that slavery was an evil that should not be allowed to spread.

The Lincoln-Douglas debates created enormous interest in Illinois—and throughout the country when they were printed in the newspapers. They made Lincoln a national figure. True, he lost the senatorial election to Douglas. But in 1860 the Republican Party nominated Lincoln for president.

The Republicans sang a campaign song:
Old Abe Lincoln came out of the wilderness,
Out of the wilderness,
Out of the wilderness,
Old Abe Lincoln came out of the wilderness
Down in Illinois!

Lincoln won the election, and in 1861 Mary's dream of living in the White House became a reality.

The new president took the oath of office on March 4, 1861. South Carolina, Mississippi, Florida, Alabama, Georgia, Louisiana, and Texas—knowing his opposition to slavery—had already seceded from the Union. South Carolina declared that "the union now subsisting between South Carolina and the other States, under the name of the 'United States of America,' is hereby dissolved."

Lincoln tried to satisfy the South by saying in his Inaugural Address that his main concern was to save the Union, not to end slavery in the states where it existed. But he added that he would enforce national laws in all the states.

Southerners were, for the most part, not satisfied by what Lincoln said. They remembered his "house divided" speech of only two years before. In that speech Lincoln quoted the Bible: "A house divided against itself cannot stand." Then he added: "I believe this government cannot endure permanently half slave and half free. I do not expect the Union to be dissolved. I do not expect the house to fall; but I do expect it will cease to be divided."

Lincoln faced a more difficult situation than any other American president has had to deal with. Some of the slave states were in secession. If he used force to bring them back into the Union, other slave states were threatening to secede. If he did not use force, the Union would be dissolved.

What was the president to do?

The Civil War

The first problem concerned Fort Sumter in the harbor of Charleston, South Carolina. Fort Sumter belonged to the United States. South Carolina claimed it and called on the garrison to surrender. Lincoln ordered the garrison to stand fast. Southern guns blasted Fort Sumter, and the commander gave up on April 13, 1861.

The firing on Fort Sumter started the Civil War.

Virginia, Arkansas, Tennessee, and North Carolina now seceded. Four slave states remained loyal to the Union—Delaware, Maryland, Kentucky, and Missouri. The western part of Virginia broke away and formed the state of West Virginia rather than leave the Union.

The seceding states formed the Confederacy, with its capital first in Montgomery, Alabama, and then in Richmond, Virginia. Jefferson Davis of Mississippi became president of the Confederacy. Robert E. Lee became its best general and the real hero of the South. Lee disliked slavery and disapproved of secession, but he remained loyal to his home state of Virginia.

The first clash in arms occurred at Bull Run in Virginia. The Northern army under General Irvin McDowell, moving forward in expectation of a quick victory, was defeated and driven back in a disorderly rout. Thomas Jonathan Jackson of the Confederate army earned his nickname—"Stonewall" Jackson—by standing firm with his men against an enemy attack.

President Lincoln was bitterly disappointed by the defeat at Bull Run. But he quickly recovered and took control of the war.

"There is no sense in crying over spilt milk," he said to William H. Seward, his Secretary of State. "I've had disappointments before, and I've learned never to despair."

"What will you do now, Mr. President?" Seward inquired.

"I'll try to find a general who can win this war. Meanwhile, you'll have to fight the war on the diplomatic front."

Lincoln meant that Confederate agents were looking for allies in Britain. Seward had to foil the Confederate agents if he could. This was difficult because British manufacturers wanted Southern cotton, and they tended to favor the Confederacy. Seward had to apologize to the London government when a Union warship removed two Confederate agents from a British ship. Lincoln finally solved the problem of British support for the Confederacy when he issued the Emancipation Proclamation.

Lincoln, hoping he had found a winning general, named General John Pope to command another invasion of Virginia. Pope got as far as Bull Run, where he suffered a shattering defeat at the hands of Lee and Jackson.

"Imagine, a second disaster in the same place!" Lincoln said to the members of his Cabinet. "Still, we can't lose heart. The Union must be preserved no matter what the cost!"

The war was taking its toll on the president. Tears came to his eyes as he read the list of dead and wounded. He felt conscience-stricken at the thought of the young men he would have to send into future battles. But there was nothing else he could

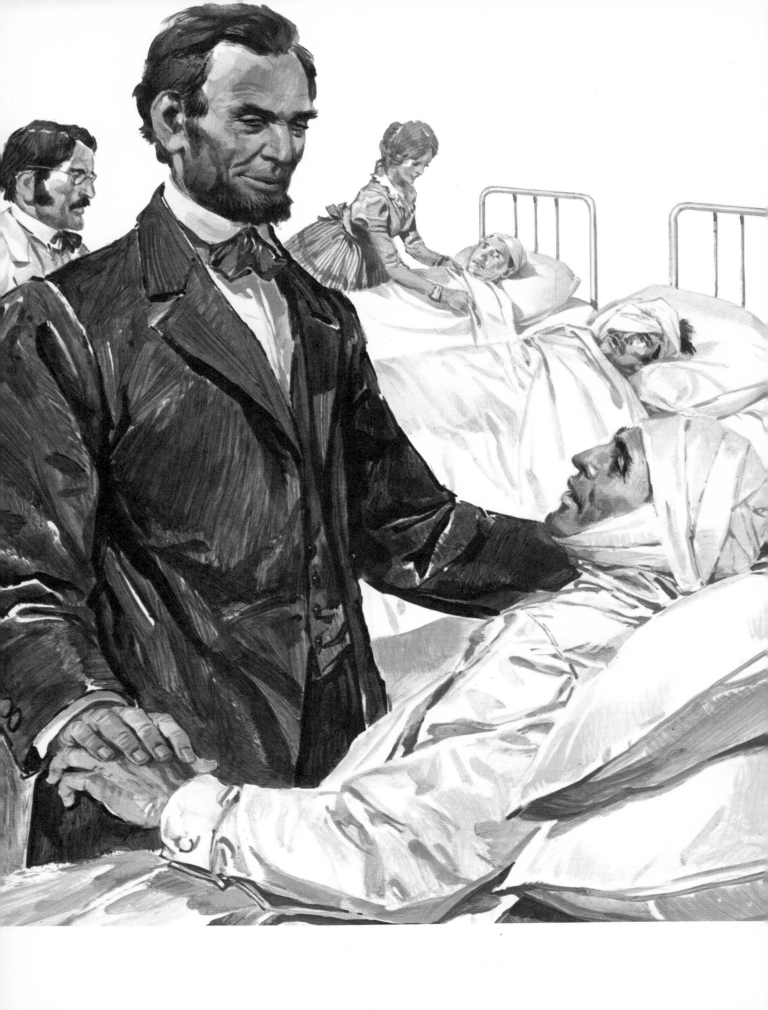

do, for the only way to save the Union was to continue the war. He never gave a thought to the possibility of surrendering to the Confederacy.

Lincoln's face showed deep, rugged furrows. The sensitive lines at the corners of his mouth became more pronounced. He frowned more frequently, for his thoughts were so often of the war and how badly it was going. Formerly clean-shaven, he now wore the beard that is so familiar to us in the photographs that were taken of him during the Civil War.

Once when Lincoln told a joke, somebody said it was no time for humor.

He replied: "If I didn't have a little humor once in a while, this war would kill me."

Despite the agonies he suffered, President Lincoln showed an extraordinary amount of energy during the war. He traveled to field hospitals to visit the wounded, thanking them, encouraging them, and making them feel that their sacrifice was not in vain.

As the war went on, Lincoln became convinced that before it ended he should free the slaves. He issued the first draft of his Emancipation Proclamation on September 23, 1862, following the Battle of Antietam. The battle was a draw between the Northern and Southern forces, but the president decided to make the most of the fact that the South had *not* won. He declared all slaves free in states in rebellion against the United States as of January 1, 1863.

"I would have preferred a victory," he admitted to Edwin M. Stanton, his Secretary of War. "But Antietam will do. I won't wait any longer to hit slavery hard."

The words came back to him that he had spoken so long ago in the New Orleans slave market.

The President had to endure more disappointments as the fighting went on. General George B. McClellan was blamed for letting Lee escape at Antietam. Lincoln now named General Ambrose E. Burnside to the top command, and Lee crushed Burnside at Fredericksburg. General Joseph Hooker came next.

Lincoln gave Hooker 130,000 men to attack Lee, who had less than 60,000. The two armies collided at Chancellorsville. Lee attacked the Union center, while Jackson made a lightning march through the woods and hit the Union right. Hooker's army broke and fled. But the Confederates suffered too because Jackson was accidentally shot and killed by his own sentries.

The war was taking its toll on the South. The North had an overwhelming advantage in manpower and industrial resources. In time, the North could wear the South down. Therefore, the South needed a quick and decisive victory.

That was the thinking behind Lee's Gettysburg Campaign. The Confederate general decided to carry the war into the North. He moved his Army of Northern Virginia up the Shenandoah Valley, crossed the Potomac River, and invaded Pennsylvania.

Lincoln appointed General George C. Meade to command the Army of the Potomac confronting the invaders.

Lincoln's instructions to Meade were short and to the point: "General Meade, I have given you all the men and guns I can. Use them to drive General Lee out of Pennsylvania. If he gets any farther north, we will be in danger of losing the war."

"Mr. President, the Army of the Potomac will do its duty," Meade responded.

"I'm sure it will, general. And I have faith in you."

The two armies approached one another in the vicinity of Gettysburg. A battle began that lasted three days, July 1, 2, and 3, 1863.

On the first day, the Confederates drove the Union forces back to defensive positions on Cemetery Ridge and Culp's Hill.

On the second day, there was a mass of confused fighting with losses on both sides.

On the third day, the decisive event of the battle took place. Lee ordered an assault on Cemetery Ridge, the strongest part of Meade's defense. The Union defenders shattered the assault.

Lee held his troops where they were until the following day. Then, realizing that the battle was lost, he retreated.

The Battle of Gettysburg remains the best-known armed conflict in American history. It was the turning point of the Civil War. The fear of defeat vanished in the North. And Southerners knew they had lost a great gamble at Gettysburg.

More good news for the North came from the West. Even as Lee retreated from Gettysburg, General Ulysses S. Grant entered Vicksburg, opening the Mississippi River to the armed forces of the Union.

On November 19, 1863, President Lincoln traveled to Gettysburg to speak at dedication ceremonies in honor of the dead. This is another reason why the Battle of Gettysburg is memorable, for Lincoln delivered one of the greatest speeches of all time—the Gettysburg Address.

The President spoke a few single words. He began by mentioning the origin of the United States in liberty and equality at the time of the Declaration of Independence. He noted that a war was going on to see whether those noble ideals could be saved. He spoke eloquently of the men who died in the Battle of Gettysburg. And he concluded by pledging that "government of the people, by the people, for the people, shall not perish from the earth."

When Lincoln finished speaking, there was only a little applause. Most of the crowd on the battlefield did not realize he had finished speaking. The speaker before him, Edward Everett, had taken two hours. Lincoln took two minutes. No wonder his audience was disappointed!

Lincoln returned from Gettysburg to the White House feeling ill. He suffered from a mild attack of smallpox. This was a contagious and dreaded disease. Consequently, those who once came to the White House asking for jobs now avoided it.

"I now have something I can give to everybody," the President joked.

Confined to his bed, he followed the war as dispatches and telegrams came in. Good news still arrived from Grant, who won the Battle of Chattanooga.

The Southern armies were being pushed back in Tennessee. But Lee was still at large in Virginia.

Lincoln decided Ulysses S. Grant was the general he had been looking for. He raised Grant to the supreme command of the Union armies.

Grant was a West Point graduate who served with distinction in the Mexican War. He left the Army in 1854, tried farming and real estate in St. Louis, and served as a clerk in his father's store in Galena, Illinois.

Returning to the Army at the outbreak of the Civil War, he forced unconditional surrender on the Confederates in Fort Donelson—after which he was known as "Unconditional Surrender" Grant. He was ready when President Lincoln gave him the responsibility for defeating Robert E. Lee.

Brothers and Sisters, Be Free!

On January 1, 1863, Abraham Lincoln signed the final version of the Emancipation Proclamation. It was afternoon in the White House with a few members of the Cabinet and other government officials present.

Lincoln sat at his desk. He had spent the morning shaking hands with a long line of visitors to the White House. Consequently, his right hand was swollen. It shook as he lifted the quill pen from the inkwell to sign the document. He paused, placed his hand on the desk, and looked at the others.

"I have never been more sure of doing what is right," he explained, "but if my signature shows that my hand trembled as I wrote, people will say I had doubts about freeing the slaves. I want to be sure that doesn't happen."

He then signed the Emancipation Proclamation with a firm hand.

The document stated that all slaves would be forever free in the areas still in rebellion against the government of the United States. It invited former slaves to join the armed forces of the Union. And it asked slaves not to rise against their masters in a bloody revolt.

At the end, Lincoln asked for "the considerate judgment of mankind, and the gracious favor of Almighty God."

The Emancipation Proclamation had little immediate effect in the rebellious areas. The slaves were still under the control of their masters and, therefore, unable to take advantage of the offer of freedom.

The big change came when Union forces advanced into the Confederacy. Slaves fled from their masters to meet the invaders. Black men accepted the offer to become soldiers of the United States. Nearly two hundred thousand joined up.

Black women sought safety behind the Union lines. Many brought children with them. They moved along with the armies for fear that if they lagged behind, they might be seized and returned to slavery.

The greatest spectacle of a black flight to the Union lines took place in Georgia in 1864. General William Tecumseh Sherman made his "March to the Sea," cutting a wide path of destruction from Atlanta to the Atlantic Ocean. He burned buildings, smashed factories, looted warehouses, broke down bridges, and tore up railroad tracks. He allowed his men to forage everywhere. They emptied barns of grain and livestock, and pilfered whatever took their fancy in the big houses of the well-to-do.

All along the route of the March to the Sea, slaves broke away from their servitude. Sherman welcomed them and gave them his protection.

Lincoln realized that freeing the slaves created problems. He therefore invited a number of free black men to the White House to discuss the future.

"I want your help in making a success of my policy," he told them.

"How can we do that, Mr. President?" asked one of his guests.

"By bringing harmony between the races. I hope whites and blacks will live in peace and equality when the war is over."

"We hope so too, Mr. President. And with you in the White House, we think it can be done."

The tragedy, of course, is that Lincoln did not live to control events after the war. He did leave a legacy of ideas that influenced the twentieth century when the Civil Rights movement began.

His eloquent words are often quoted: "In giving freedom to the slave, we assure freedom to the free—honorable alike in what we give, and what we preserve. We shall nobly save, or meanly lose, the last best hope of the earth."

The Emancipation Proclamation gave Abraham Lincoln the title of the Great Emancipator. That is how we still remember him.

Lincoln thought of it as a moral document, but it also proved to be a stroke of political genius. When he freed the slaves, he destroyed sympathy for the Confederacy in Europe. No government would any longer ally itself with a system based on slavery. Sympathy shifted to the Union in its effort to put down a pro-slavery rebellion.

The war was not over when Lincoln signed the Emancipation Proclamation. Indeed, the Battle of Gettysburg was still to be fought. Nevertheless, Lincoln felt more at peace with himself than he had when the war started.

His life-long hatred of slavery had reached its climax. He had made good on his promise to "hit it hard."

When he returned to the private quarters of the president in the White House after signing the Emancipation Proclamation, Mary Todd Lincoln said: "Abraham, you look satisfied."

"I am satisfied, my dear. I only wish every day could be as satisfying as this one."

A man of both thought and action, Abraham Lincoln was fully committed to the principle that democracy is the best form of government. How is democracy to be safeguarded? By guaranteeing equal rights to all people.

It is interesting to note that Lincoln did not mean only racial equality. He meant equality of the sexes too. He wrote in one of his letters that he believed women should have the right to vote. He could not tolerate any form of privilege—political, social, or economic.

Lincoln also believed in free education for all children. Like his great predecessor, Thomas Jefferson, he thought that democracy could survive only when its citizens were well-informed, literate, and active in promoting the good of their nation. In particular, they must know how to choose able, honest leaders.

Lincoln went for drives in the country with the First Lady whenever he could. He enjoyed the fresh air. The trees and bushes reminded him of his days back in Illinois. Sometimes Mary would recall their first meeting in Springfield when he was a prairie lawyer and state politician.

The coachman would soon turn the horse around, and they would return to the White House. The duties of the president were always waiting for Lincoln. He was still Commander-in-Chief of the armed forces, and the war was still on. But at last it was nearing an end.

Under the command of Ulysses S. Grant, the Grand Army of the Republic pushed south into Virginia. His objective was Richmond, the Confederate capital.

Robert E. Lee fought brilliant defensive battles. He forced Grant to take thousands of casualties in the wilderness and at Spotsylvania, Cold Harbor, and Petersburg. However, Grant could afford the losses because of his enormous superiority in manpower. Lee could not afford his smaller number of casualties because he had almost no replacements for the men he lost.

While Grant was driving toward Richmond, Lincoln completed his first term in the White House. In the election of 1864, George B. McClellan ran as the candidate of the Democratic Party. Lincoln, again heading the Republican ticket, won the election.

"Abraham, this shows your popularity!" Mary Todd Lincoln exclaimed.

"Well, it also shows the popularity of my generals. They're winning the war for me. The people know what Grant and Sherman are doing. So, the people don't want any change until the war is over. They don't want to change horses in the middle of the stream."

In his Second Inaugural Address, Lincoln looked forward to the end of the Civil War. He spoke these well-known words: "With malice toward none; with charity for all; with firmness in the right, as God gives us to see the right—let us strive on to finish the work we are in: to bind up the nation's wounds; to care for him who shall have borne the battle, and for his widow and his orphan; to do all which may achieve and cherish a just and lasting peace among ourselves, and with all nations."

On April 9, 1865, Lee surrendered to Grant at Appomattox Court House in Virginia. The Civil War was over.

Lincoln had achieved the two main goals of his life. He had freed the slaves, and he had saved the Union. He no longer had to carry the burden of the war. He visited Richmond, where a crowd of former slaves cheered him through the streets. This was an emotional experience for him.

It was almost Easter. Lincoln looked forward to a quiet holiday in the company of Mary and their sons, Robert and Tad.

On the morning of Good Friday, April 14, 1865, Lincoln met the members of his cabinet. They discussed plans for his second Administration. They concentrated on the problems of reorganizing state governments in the former Confederacy. Lincoln's hope was to see the South restored to peace and prosperity as before the Civil War—but without slavery.

On that very day, conspirators in Washington were planning to kill the president. They were led by John Wilkes Booth, an actor from Virginia. Booth, like many others in the South, hated the man responsible for the defeat of the Confederacy. Booth had his gun ready. He was waiting for a chance to get at the president.

Lincoln passed most of the afternoon peacefully at the White House. That evening, he and the First Lady, with two friends, went to Ford's Theater to see a play called *Our American Cousin*. During their life in Washington, they both enjoyed going to the theater or the opera whenever the president could spare an evening from his official duties. They and their friends were in good spirits as they drove through Washington.

At Ford's Theater they were escorted up a flight of stairs to a box draped with

flags for the occasion. The play had already started. The actors paused and bowed to the president. The audience cheered. He, the First Lady, and their guests sat down. The play resumed.

Our American Cousin was a light comedy, popular at the time. Soon all those in the president's box, including his bodyguard from the White House, were caught up in the action onstage. The First Lady noticed that the president was enjoying himself. She leaned over and placed her hand on his.

Meanwhile, John Wilkes Booth was lurking near the theater. He had seen Lincoln go in. This was, for Booth, the moment to strike.

The third act of the play was going on when Booth entered the theater and made his way to the president's box. Nobody who saw him suspected anything. He entered the box, pulled out a revolver, and shot Lincoln in the back of the head. Lincoln slumped forward in his chair.

Booth leaped from the box onto the stage, tripping and breaking his leg as he did so. He shouted "Sic Semper Tyrannis!" ("Thus Ever to Tyrants!"), the motto of Virginia. Then he limped away and escaped. Eventually, however, his pursuers caught up with the assassin and shot him.

Gravely injured, Lincoln was carried to a house across the street. Doctors, hurriedly called in, fought to save his life. He died at 7:22 on the morning of April 15, 1865.

The news caused expressions of grief throughout the country, not least among Southerners who knew he would have been fair to the South.

On April 19, a long funeral procession took Lincoln's body from the White House to the Capitol, where it lay in state as thousands of mourners passed by to pay their last respects to the president who saved the Union. The procession of men and women, black and white, went on for two days.

On April 22, a special train set out from Washington. It carried the mortal remains of Abraham Lincoln to Springfield, Illinois. At each station, crowds came out to bid the president goodbye. Millions of Americans watched the funeral train pass. They realized they had lost a very great man.

Secretary of War Stanton made a fitting comment just after Lincoln died: "Now he belongs to the ages."

Abraham Lincoln may well have been America's greatest president. He faced and overcame the greatest crisis of American history—secession and civil war. He filled the office of the president with dignity. He made ordinary citizens feel that he was one of them.

No other president ever spoke as eloquently as he did. None ever wrote such memorable prose. His words—from the Lincoln-Douglas debates, the Gettysburg Address, the Second Inaugural Address—are part of American literature.

Such was the heritage of Abraham Lincoln. It is a heritage we all share.

The Lincoln Memorial

The Lincoln Memorial was built in Washington, D.C. to honor Abraham Lincoln, the sixteenth president of the United States. Work began on the monument on February 12, 1915, when the cornerstone was laid, and concluded when the building was dedicated in May, 1922. It was designed by Henry Bacon.

The building is made of marble and consists of a center hall which houses a huge statue of Lincoln by Daniel Chester French. On the outside of the building are 36 columns, representing the thirty six states which comprised the Union when Lincoln died in 1865.

The text of Lincoln's Gettysburg Address and his Second Inaugural Address are inscribed on tablets inside the memorial.

Lincoln's Gettysburg Address

The Gettysburg Address is undoubtedly Lincoln's most famous speech. He delivered it on November 19, 1863. The occasion was the dedication ceremony for the cemetery at Gettysburg, the site of the Civil War battle where 5,000 men lost their lives. The speech was printed and soon became known as a classic. Its fame spread wherever the English language was spoken, at home and abroad. Countless school children have memorized the Gettysburg Address throughout the years.

Four score and seven years ago our fathers brought forth on this continent a new nation, conceived in liberty and dedicated to the proposition that all men are created equal.

Now we are engaged in a great civil war, testing whether that nation, or any nation so conceived and so dedicated, can long endure. We are met on a great battlefield of that war. We have come to dedicate a portion of that field, as a final resting place for those who here gave their lives that that nation might live. It is altogether fitting and proper that we should do this.

But, in a larger sense, we cannot dedicate—we cannot consecrate—we cannot hallow—this ground. The brave men, living and dead, who struggled here, have consecrated it, far above our poor power to add or detract. The world will little note nor long remember what we say here, but it can never forget what they did here. It is for us the living, rather, to be dedicated here to the unfinished work which they who fought here have thus far so nobly advanced. It is rather for us to be here dedicated to the great task remaining before us—that from these honored dead we take increased devotion to that cause for which they gave the last full measure of devotion—that we here highly resolve that these dead shall not have died in vain—that this nation, under God, shall have a new birth of freedom—and that government of the people, by the people, for the people, shall not perish from the earth.

Abraham Lincoln
November 19, 1863

The Emancipation Proclamation

In September of 1862 Lincoln announced to members of his Cabinet his plan to free the slaves. This plan became known as the Emancipation Proclamation, and Lincoln formally issued it on January 1, 1863. Up until this point in the war Lincoln's main concern had not been to free the slaves, but to reunite the two halves of the country:

My paramount object in this struggle is to save the Union, and is not either to save or destroy slavery. If I could save the Union without freeing any slave I would do it; and if I could save it by freeing all the slaves, I would do it; and if I could do it by freeing some and leaving others alone, I would also do that.

As president he felt that holding the Union together was his obligation. Personally, though, he wanted to end slavery. When he was able to finally sign the Emancipation Proclamation, he felt a great sense of accomplishment saying "I never in my life felt more certain that I was doing right than I do in signing this paper."

That on the 1st day of January, A.D. 1863, all persons held as slaves within any State or designated part of a State the people whereof shall then be in rebellion against the United States shall be then, thenceforward, and forever free; and the executive government of the United States including the military and naval authority thereof, will recognize and maintain the freedom of such persons and will do no act or acts to repress such persons, or any of them, in any efforts they may make for their actual freedom.

That the executive will on the 1st day of January aforesaid, by proclamation, designate the States and parts of States, if any, in which the people thereof, respectively, shall then be in rebellion against the United States...

...I do order and declare that all persons held as slaves within said designated States and parts of States are, and henceforward shall be free...

And I hereby enjoin upon the people so declared to be free to abstain from all violence, unless in necessary self-defense; and I recommend to them that, in all cases when allowed, they labor faithfully for reasonable wages.

...And upon this act, sincerely believed to be an act of justice, warranted by the Constitution upon military necessity, I invoke the considerate judgement of mankind and the gracious favor of Almighty God."

From the Emancipation Proclamation

Picking cotton in Mississippi

Greeting from Garibaldi to Lincoln

The historic Emancipation Proclamation of the United States was applauded throughout the world and won the admiration of people fighting to be free everywhere.

Among the first statements of the Italian liberator, Giuseppe Garibaldi, is this open letter to President Lincoln, dated August 14, 1863.

TO ABRAHAM LINCOLN, EMANCIPATOR OF THE SLAVES OF THE UNITED STATES OF AMERICA.

If, in the midst of your titanic battles, you are to lend an ear for a moment to our voices, Oh Lincoln, know that we, the free sons of Columbus send you our congratulations for the great work you have achieved.

Shaped by the thought of Christ and of Brown, you will pass into History under the name of Emancipator, a name more enviable than any royal title, than any other treasure. Because of you and the noble blood shed by Americans, an entire race has been freed from the egotistical yoke of slavery and dignity has been restored to mankind.

America, the mistress of Liberty, has opened a new age in the solemn progress of mankind. The world now wages a sad and bitter struggle for equality, and you have shown the way.

We celebrate the destruction of slavery!

We salute you, Abraham Lincoln, captain of the ship of freedom! We salute all those who have been freed and we, the free men of Italy, kiss the iron links of your chains.

The Liberals of Italy

Giuseppe Garibaldi

The Expedition of the "Thousand": the debarkation of Garibaldi at Marsala.

O Captain! My Captain

Like any great human benefactor Abraham Lincoln inspired authors and poets, artists and sculptors. One particularly significant work is this poem by Walt Whitman written in memory of President Lincoln's assassination.

O Captain! my Captain! our fearful trip is done,
The ship has weather'd every rack, the prize we sought is won,
The port is near, the bells I hear, the people all exulting,
While follow eyes the steady keel, the vessel grim and daring;
But O heart! heart! heart!
O the bleeding drops of red,
Where on the deck my Captain lies,
Fallen cold and dead.

O Captain! my Captain! rise up and hear the bells;
Rise up—for you the flag is flung—for you the bugle trills,
For you bouquets and ribbon'd wreaths—for you the shores acrowding,
For you they call, the swaying mass, their eager faces turning;
Here Captain! dear father!
The arm beneath your head!
It is some dream that on the deck,
You've fallen cold and dead.

My Captain does not answer, his lips are pale and still,
My father does not feel my arm, he has no pulse nor will,
The ship is anchor'd safe and sound, its voyage closed and done,
From fearful trip the victor ship comes in with object won;
Exult O shores, and ring O bells!
But I with mournful tread,
Walk the deck my Captain lies,
Fallen cold and dead.

Painting of Walt Whitman by William Smith

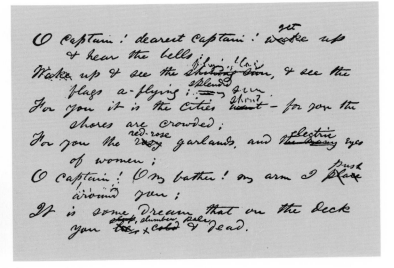

Manuscript of Walt Whitman's poem written in memory of Lincoln: "O Captain! My Captain!"

Acts on Human Rights

The Declaration of Independence issued July 4, 1776 inspired feelings for liberty in countries other than our own by stating our natural and unalienable human rights, and the obligations of governments to protect these rights. In fact, the French expressed the same sentiments and ideas in somewhat different words in their Declaration of the Rights of Man, a prefix to their constitution of 1791.

"...We hold these truths to be self evident; that all men are created equal, that they are endowed by their creator with certain unalienable rights, that among these are life, liberty, and the pursuit of happiness. That to secure these rights, governments are instituted among men, deriving their just powers from the consent of the governed; that whenever any form of government becomes destructive of these ends, it is the right of people to alter or to abolish it, and to institute new government, laying its foundation on such principles, and organizing its powers in such form, as to them shall seem most likely to effect their safety and happiness."

from The Declaration of Independence

In June of 1788 the Constitution of the United States went into effect creating a federal government. The Constitution gave the United States government powers over the individual states.

...The citizens of each State shall be entitled to all privileges and immunities of citizens of the several states

...No person held to service or labor in the State, under the laws thereof, escaping into another, shall, in consequence of any law or regulation therein, be discharged from such service or labor, but shall be delivered up on claim of the party to whom such service or labor may be due.

From Article IV, Section 2
The Constitution of the U.S.A.

In 1865, shortly after the end of the Civil War, the Thirteenth Amendment was added to the Constitution. It changed Article IV of the Constitution by prohibiting slavery. The government was also given the power to pass laws to enforce the amendment.

Neither slavery nor involuntary servitude, except as a punishment for crime whereof the party shall have been duly convicted, shall exist within the United States, or any place subject to their jurisdiction.

Amendment 13
The Constitution of the U.S.A.

The Universal Declaration of Human Rights was approved on December 10, 1948, by the General Assembly of the United Nations. Although no provisions were made by the Assembly to enforce the terms of the declaration, it has still served a purpose as a directive to the world on moral principles.

The General Assembly

Proclaims this Universal Declaration of Human Rights as a common standard of achievement for all people and all nations to the end that every individual and every organ of society, keeping this declaration constantly in mind, shall strive by teaching and education to promote respect for these rights and freedoms and by progressive measures, both national and international, to secure their universal and effective recognition and observance...

...Everyone is entitled to all the rights and freedoms set forth in this Declaration, without distinction of any kind, such as race, colour, sex, language, religion, political or other opinion, national or social origin, property, birth, or other status.

...No one shall be held in slavery or servitude; slavery and the slave trade shall be prohibited in all their forms.

...Education shall be directed to the full development of the human personality and to the strengthening of respect for human rights and fundamental freedoms, it shall promote understanding, tolerance, and friendship among all nations, racial or religious groups, and shall further the activities of the United Nations for the maintenance of peace.

HISTORICAL CHRONOLOGY

The Declaration of Independence dated July 4, 1776.

Life of Lincoln	Historical and Cultural Events
	1774 Philadelphia Declaration of Rights
	1776 July 4—Declaration of Independence
	1783 The 13 colonies become the United States
	1789 French revolution
	1804 Napoleon Bonaparte declares himself Emperor
	1805 Death of Johann Christoph Schiller, who with Goethe, was greatest German writer
1809 Lincoln is born in Hodgensville, KY, February 12	
	1814 Napoleon abdicates
	1815 Congress of Vienna divides Europe
1816 Lincoln's family moves to Indiana	
1818 Lincoln's mother dies	
1819/ 1825 Lincoln works at many jobs and studies law	

The Congress of Vienna—present are the five great powers of Europe.

Raftsmen Playing Cards—George Caleb Bingham

Engraving of an insurrection at Palermo, Italy, in 1820.

Life of Lincoln	Historical and Cultural Events
	1820 First Italian national rebellions
	1821 James Fenimore Cooper publishes *The Spy*
	1823 The Monroe Doctrine against European intervention in the Americas
	1824 Byron dies in Missolonghi, Greece, of fever while aiding rebels in the Greek fight for independence from the Turks.
	1824/ Numerous Latin American countries revolt **1830** against Spain
	1825 Erie Canal completed
1832 Unsuccessful nomination as Whig candidate	**1832** Goethe Dies
	1833 Westward expansion across the Mississippi
1834 Lincoln elected to Illinois assembly	
1836 Lincoln is admitted to bar	
	1840 Alessandro Manzoni writes the great nationalist Italian novel, *The Betrothed*

George Saunders—Painting of Lord Byron, the English writer

Simón Bolívar leads the Latin American countries in a revolt against Spain.

From the Currier and Ives Treasury: *The Rocky Mountains—Immigrants Crossing the Plains*

Tobacco growers at the Slave Market in Virginia—1819

Life of Lincoln	Historical and Cultural Events
1842 Leaves the assembly	
1846 Elected to Congress	**1846/** Mexican War **1838**
1849 Presents first plan for abolition of slavery/criticizes President Polk for useless war against Mexico Leaves Congress and returns to private practice	**1849** California Gold Rush Constitution of Frankfurt for the Unification of Germany
	1849/ War of Independence for **1859** the unification of Italy
	1850 The music of the Italian composer and patriot, Giuseppe Verdi, becomes identified with the Italian Nationalist Movement during Italy's struggle for independence from Austria.
	1851 First London Exposition for inventions etc.
	1852 Harriet Beecher Stowe publishes *Uncle Tom's Cabin* with its anti-slavery message
1854/ Lincoln returns to politics **1856** Joins Republican party	**1854/** Crimean War—England, **1856** France and Piedmont fight with Turkey against Russia

A goldminer in his cabin—1852

A painting of the war of independence in Milan for the unification of Italy.

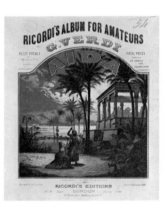

The English edition of Giuseppe Verdi's opera *Aida*

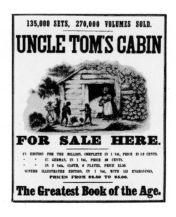

A poster advertising Harriet Beecher Stowe's *Uncle Tom's Cabin*

Life of Lincoln	Historical and Cultural Events
1860 Abraham Lincoln elected 16th president of the United States	**1860** Garibaldi leads his Thousand into Sicily
1861 The Confederate States secede from the Union	**1861** Kingdom of Italy proclaimed in Turin The Czar frees the serfs in Russia
1863 The Emancipation Proclamation, January 1 Gettysburg Address, November 19	
1864 Lincoln reelected to the presidency	**1864** The First Worker's International
1865 South surrenders unconditionally Lincoln enters Richmond, April 9 Lincoln assassinated, April 14	
	1867 Defeat of French in Mexico End of European intervention in America Franz Joseph becomes Emperor of The Austro-Hungarian Empire
	1870 Rome becomes capital of Italy

Statue of Abraham Lincoln in the Lincoln Memorial—Washington, D.C.

Embarkation of the Thousand at Quarto by T. Van Elven

The Civil War: The Battle of Gettysburg— Photograph by Matthew Brady

Portrait of Franz Joseph, emperor of the Austro-Hungarian Empire

SOURCES

Original documents:

Basler, Roy P. (ed.), *Abraham Lincoln: His Speeches and Writings* (1940)

Secondary authorities:

Anderson, David D., *Abraham Lincoln* (1970)

Longford, Lord, *Abraham Lincoln* (1975)

Sandburg, Carl, *Abraham Lincoln: The Prairie Years* (1926); *Abraham Lincoln: The War Years* (1939)

Thomas, Benjamin P., *Abraham Lincoln* (1952)

Index

2 3 4 5 6 7 8 9 10—IL—93 92 91 90 89 88 87 86